Symm

Jack Beers

Addison Wesley

Toronto

This is a lemur.
Look at the left half of its face.
Look at the right half.
Are the two halves alike?

This is half of a ladybug.
What does the other half
look like?
Hold a mirror
along the line to see.

The ladybug has spots on both halves.
The ladybug is symmetrical.
Both sides are the same size.
Both sides have the same parts.

This half of a dragonfly has two wings.
How many wings does the dragonfly have in all?
Use the mirror to see.

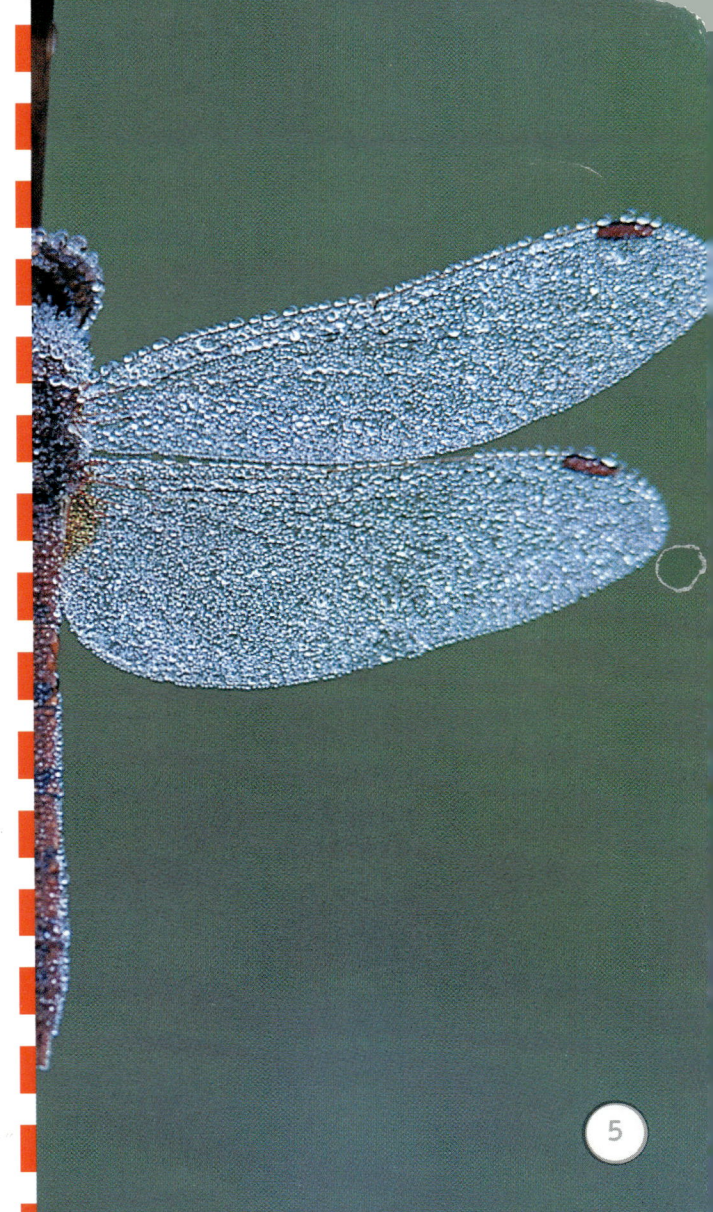

There are four wings in all.
The dragonfly is symmetrical, too.

This half
of a crab
has four legs,
one eye,
and one claw.
How many legs,
eyes, and claws
does the crab
have in all?

The whole crab has eight legs,
two eyes, and two claws.
If four legs point left,
how many legs point right?
What other parts point left or right?

The spider
is symmetrical, too.
What is the same
about each side?
What is different?

Each side has four legs and one eye.
On one side the legs point left.
On the other side they point right.

Here is a lizard and its reflection.
Are the lizard and its reflection symmetrical?
How are they the same?
How are they different?

The frog sees its reflection in the water.
Hold the mirror along the line.
The line is called a line of symmetry.
Can you find a second line of symmetry?

This is a starfish.
Count the points.
Hold the mirror along the line of symmetry.
Can you find more lines of symmetry?

The starfish has five lines of symmetry.

This is a diatom. It lives in water and is very small. How many lines of symmetry can you find?

Every line through the centre of the diatom is a line of symmetry.

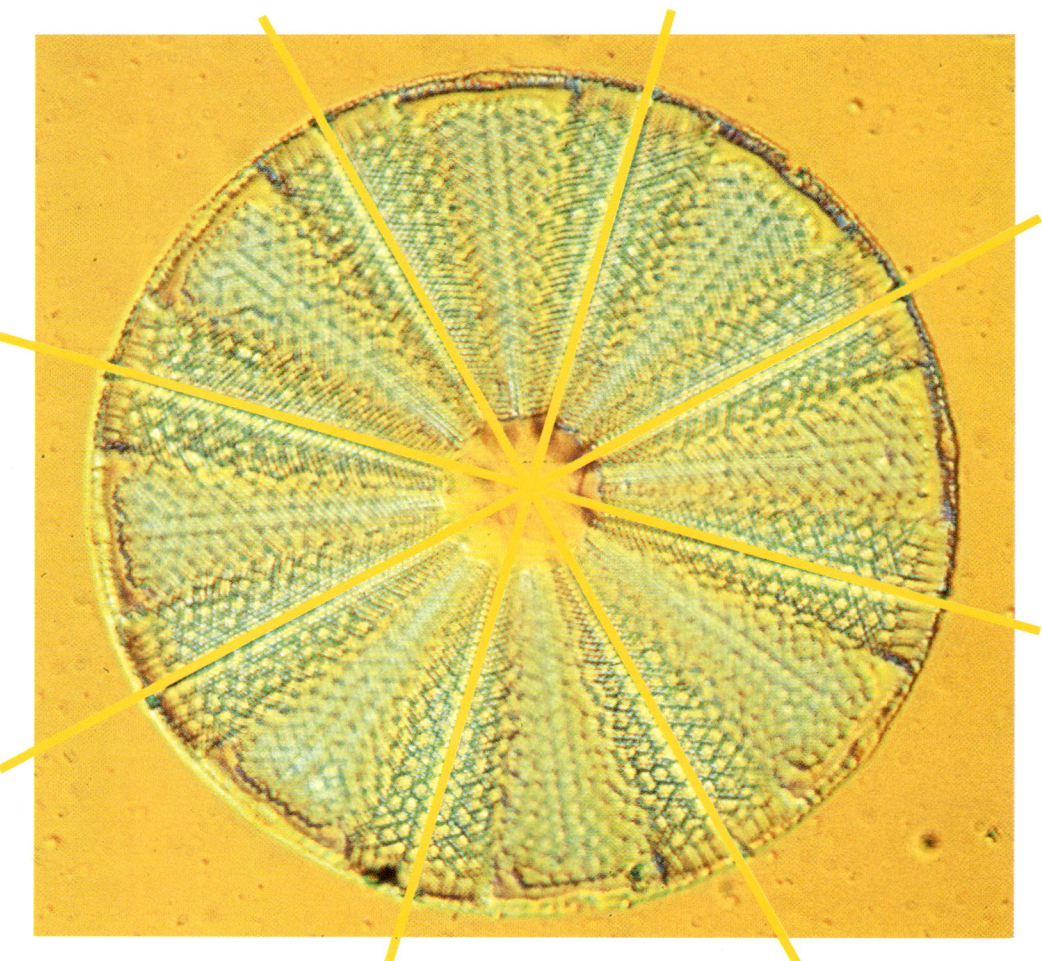